What kind of living thing is it?

Bobbie Kalman

Crabtree Publishing Company

www.crabtreebooks.com

D1211645

Created by Bobbie Kalman

Dedicated by Kathy Middleton
For Rob

**Author and
Editor-in-Chief**
Bobbie Kalman

Editor
Kathy Middleton

Proofreader
Crystal Sikkens

Design
Bobbie Kalman
Katherine Berti

**Production coordinator
and Prepress technician**
Katherine Berti

Photo research
Bobbie Kalman

Illustrations
Katherine Berti: pages 6 and 24 (skeleton)
Bonna Rouse: page 6 (bear)

Photographs
iStockPhoto: page 18 (cat and mouse)
Other photographs by Shutterstock

Library and Archives Canada Cataloguing in Publication

Kalman, Bobbie, 1947-
    What kind of living thing is it? / Bobbie Kalman.

(Introducing living things)
Includes index.
Issued also in an electronic format.
ISBN 978-0-7787-3235-8 (bound).--ISBN 978-0-7787-3259-4 (pbk.)

    1. Organisms--Juvenile literature. 2. Life (Biology)--Juvenile
literature. I. Title. II. Series.

QH309.2.K255 2011   j578   C2010-903018-4

Library of Congress Cataloging-in-Publication Data

Kalman, Bobbie.
  What kind of living thing is it? / Bobbie Kalman.
       p. cm. -- (Introducing living things)
  Includes index.
  ISBN 978-0-7787-3259-4 (pbk. : alk. paper) -- ISBN 978-0-7787-3235-8
(reinforced library binding : alk. paper) -- ISBN 978-1-4271-9491-6
(electronic)
  1. Organisms--Juvenile literature. 2. Life (Biology)--Juvenile literature.
I. Title. II. Series.

  QH309.2.K26 2010
  570--dc22
                                                    2010018037

Crabtree Publishing Company

Printed in China/082010/AP20100512

www.crabtreebooks.com   1-800-387-7650

**Published in Canada
Crabtree Publishing**
616 Welland Ave.
St. Catharines, Ontario
L2M 5V6

**Published in the United States
Crabtree Publishing**
PMB 59051
350 Fifth Avenue, 59th Floor
New York, New York 10118

**Published in the United Kingdom
Crabtree Publishing**
Maritime House
Basin Road North, Hove
BN41 1WR

**Published in Australia
Crabtree Publishing**
386 Mt. Alexander Rd.
Ascot Vale (Melbourne)
VIC 3032

Contents

What is a living thing?

What is a **living thing**? Plants are living things. Animals are living things. People are living things. There are other kinds of living things, too. Which kinds of living things do you know?

snake

butterfly

snail

frog

Living things are different in many ways, but they are also the same in many ways.

fish

plant

bird

How are living things the same? Living things need air, water, and food. Most living things also need sunshine. Living things grow, change, and move. They make other living things.

chipmunk

Living things make babies or other living things like themselves. This mother horse has a baby horse that will grow and change.

Animal bodies

Animals are living things. Some animals have **backbones** inside their bodies. Backbones are a row of bones in the middle of an animal's back. All the bones make up a **skeleton**. Animals with backbones are called **vertebrates**.

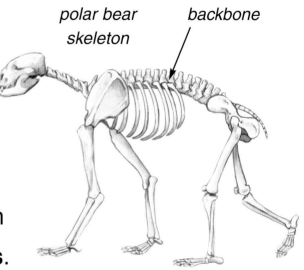

polar bear skeleton

backbone

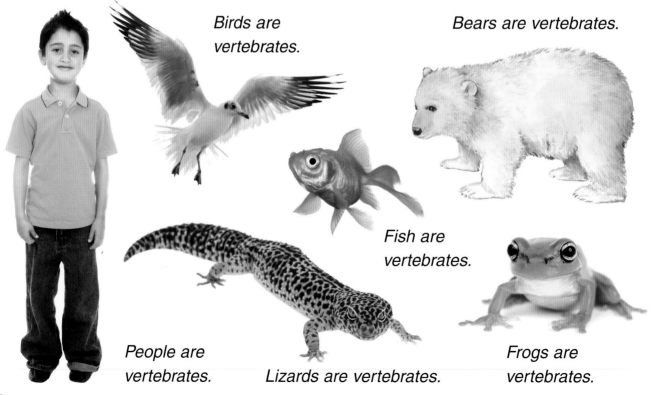

Birds are vertebrates.

Bears are vertebrates.

Fish are vertebrates.

People are vertebrates.

Lizards are vertebrates.

Frogs are vertebrates.

Some animals have backbones, but most animals have no backbones. Animals without backbones are called **invertebrates**. Invertebrates live in water and on land.

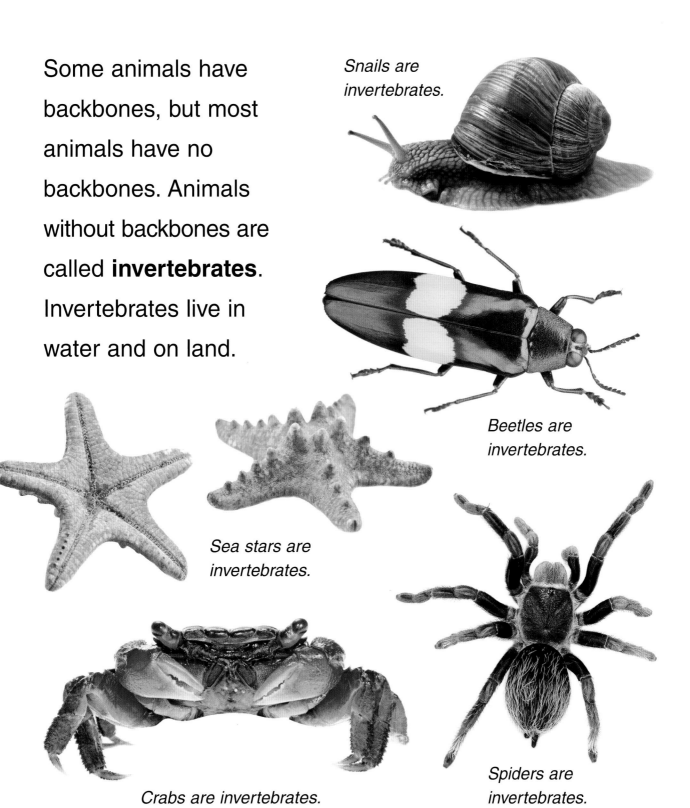

Snails are invertebrates.

Beetles are invertebrates.

Sea stars are invertebrates.

Spiders are invertebrates.

Crabs are invertebrates.

Which are insects?

1. Are crabs insects? They have eight legs that bend.

Arthropods are invertebrates with legs that bend. Insects, spiders, and crabs have legs that bend. Insects are arthropods with six legs. Many insects also have wings. Some of the arthropods shown here are insects. How many insects did you find?

spider

fly

2. Is a spider an insect? How many legs does it have? Is a fly an insect?

4. Is a butterfly an insect? Count its legs.

3. Is this an insect or a leaf? Why do you think so?

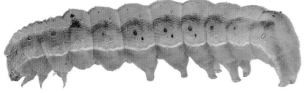

real legs

5. Caterpillars have six real legs. Are they insects?

antennae

6. Are ants insects?

Answers

1. Crabs are not insects.
2. Spiders have eight legs. They are not insects, but flies are insects.
3. This leaf insect is an insect that looks like a leaf.
4. Butterflies are insects.
5. Caterpillars become butterflies. They are insects.
6. Ants have six legs and two antennae. They are insects.

What are reptiles?

Reptiles are animals with backbones. Some reptiles live on land, and some live in water. All reptiles have **scales**, and most reptiles **hatch** from, or come out of, eggs. Some reptiles have four legs and a tail. Some reptiles have no legs. Two kinds of reptiles have shells. Find the animal on these two pages that is not a reptile.

These baby crocodiles are hatching from eggs. Are they reptiles?

scales

*A turtle has
four legs and a tail.
It also has a shell on its back.*

*A snake has scales all over
its body. It has no legs.*

salamander

The salamander has moist skin that makes
mucus, or slime. It does not have scales.

*A lizard has four legs,
a long tail, and scales.*

Crocodiles, turtles, lizards,
and snakes are reptiles. The
salamander is not a reptile.
It is an amphibian. Learn about
amphibians on pages 12–13.

Living two lives

Amphibians are animals that start their lives in water and live on land when they are adults. Frogs, toads, newts, and salamanders are amphibians. Amphibians breathe through **gills** when they start their lives in water. They breathe with **lungs** when they are adults.

gills

*This newt **larva**, or young newt, will live underwater until it is an adult. It breathes through gills, which are behind its head. As an adult, the newt will live on land and breathe with lungs.*

Some frogs live in trees. Other frogs live on the ground close to water.

Salamanders and newts are amphibians that have tails. Frogs and toads do not have tails.

Toads have dry, bumpy skin and short back legs.

newt

salamander

Which is not a fish?

betta

scales

Fish are vertebrates that live in water. Some fish are small, and some are big. Most fish have scales all over their bodies. The betta on the left is a fish, but some fish do not look like this fish.

Is a moray eel a fish? It looks more like a snake!

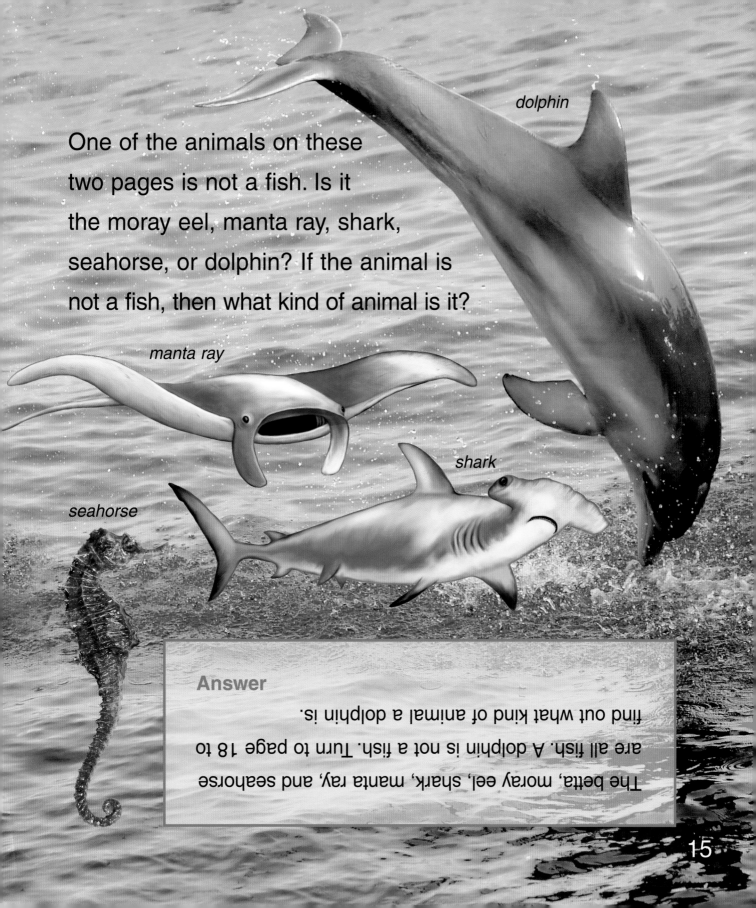

One of the animals on these two pages is not a fish. Is it the moray eel, manta ray, shark, seahorse, or dolphin? If the animal is not a fish, then what kind of animal is it?

dolphin

manta ray

shark

seahorse

Answer

The betta, moray eel, shark, manta ray, and seahorse are all fish. A dolphin is not a fish. Turn to page 18 to find out what kind of animal a dolphin is.

Is it a bird or not?

Birds are the only animals that are covered in feathers. Birds also have wings, but not all birds fly. Some birds swim, and some birds can run fast. One of the animals shown on these pages is not a bird. Which one is it? What kind of animal is it?

Penguins live in a very cold place where there is a lot of ice. They swim in oceans.

Gulls fly above oceans looking for fish to catch.

Birds hatch from eggs. Is this duck a bird?

Bats have big wings for flying. They have no feathers. Are they birds?

Emus are big animals with feathers and wings. They cannot fly, but they can run fast. Are emus birds?

Parrots have colorful feathers. Many parrots talk. Are they birds?

Answer

All the animals on pages 16 and 17, except the bat, are birds. Find out what kind of animal a bat is on page 18.

baby emus

What is a mammal?

Mammals are animals with backbones. They have hair or fur on their bodies. Bats are the only mammals that fly. Dolphins are mammals that live in oceans. They have to breathe air above water. People are mammals, too.

Elephants are the biggest mammals that live on land.

The cat and mouse above are mammals. They have backbones. They have fur on their bodies.

This girl and her dog are mammals.

Mammal babies are **born**. They do not hatch from eggs the way reptiles and birds do. Mammal mothers make milk inside their bodies for their babies to drink. Drinking mother's milk is called **nursing**. The baby polar bears below are nursing.

This baby orangutan is a mammal. It is a kind of ape.

Plants are living things

Plants are living things that make their own food. They need sunshine, air, and water, just as you do. Flowers, trees, bushes, and grass are plants. What kind of plants are in the picture below?

bushes

grass

flowers

Most plants have **roots**, **leaves**, and **stems**. Some plants have flowers and fruits. Trees are the biggest plants. They can grow in soil or water. Bushes are smaller than trees.

There are trees and many other plants in this picture. The mushrooms in the picture are not plants. Turn the page to find out what kind of living things they are.

flowers

stem

leaves

roots

21

Other living things

Plants, animals, and people are living things, but there are other kinds of living things, too. Mushrooms look like plants, but they are living things called **fungi**. Fungi cannot make food the way plants can. Mushrooms break down dead plants, such as leaves and tree bark, to get energy.

mushroom

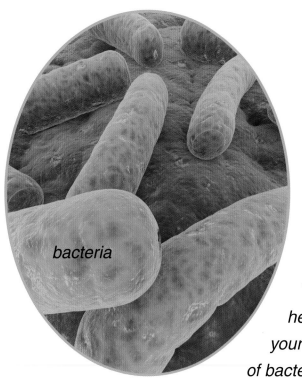

bacteria

Bacteria are among the smallest living things on Earth. You cannot see them without a microscope. You have billions of helpful bacteria inside your body, but some kinds of bacteria can make you sick.

microscope

(left) These small living things look like trees, but they are worms that live in oceans. Worms are animals.

(above) Earthworms live underground.

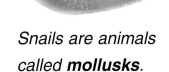

Snails are animals called **mollusks**.

Sea stars are simple ocean animals with five arms and no heads.

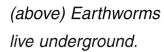

polyps

Corals live in oceans. They are made up of many tiny animals called **polyps**.

23

Words to know and Index

amphibians
pages 11,
12–13

arthropods
page 8

birds
pages 4, 6,
16–17, 19

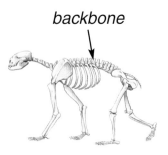

backbone

bodies
pages 6–7, 11,
14, 18, 19, 22

fish
pages 4, 6,
14–15, 16

fungi
pages 21,
22

insects
pages
8–9

Other index words

babies pages 5, 10, 19

backbones pages 6, 7,
  10, 18

bacteria page 22

eggs pages 10, 16, 19

invertebrates pages
  7, 8

mushrooms pages 21,
  22

people pages 8, 9

scales pages 10,
  11, 14

vertebrates pages 6, 14

wings pages 8, 16, 17

mammals
pages 18–19

plants
pages 4,
20–21, 22

reptiles
pages
10–11, 19